This
Bible Story Time
book belongs to

_____

_____

_____

For Lucy - E.C.

Text by Sophie Piper
Illustrations copyright © 2006 Estelle Corke
This edition copyright © 2006 Lion Hudson

The moral rights of the author and illustrator
have been asserted

A Lion Children's Book
an imprint of
Lion Hudson plc
Mayfield House, 256 Banbury Road,
Oxford OX2 7DH, England
www.lionhudson.com
ISBN-13 978 0 7459 4872 0
ISBN-10 0 7459 4872 3

First edition 2006
1 3 5 7 9 10 8 6 4 2 0

A catalogue record for this book is available
from the British Library

Typeset in 20/24 Baskerville MT Schlbk
Printed and bound in China

BIBLE STORY TIME

The First Easter

Sophie Piper * Estelle Corke

LION
CHILDREN'S

It was nearly time for the biggest festival of the year.

'Let's go to Jerusalem,' said Jesus to his friends. 'That's the best place to be at festival time.'

Jesus rode to the city on a donkey. People began to whisper. 'Look! Jesus is riding to Jerusalem. He looks like a king!'

'God bless the king!' shouted someone. Everyone began to cheer. They cut palm branches and waved them like flags.

Jesus went through the city gate
that led to the Temple.

It was like being in a marketplace.
There were even live animals for
sale.

'This is all wrong,' said Jesus
to the stallholders. 'Get out at
once!

'The Temple is meant to be
a place of prayer. You just
want to make money.'
He chased
everyone out.

The people in charge of the Temple frowned. 'Jesus is a troublemaker,' they grumbled.

'How can we get rid of him?'

Not long after, a man named Judas came to see them. He was meant to be one of Jesus' best friends. 'I can tell you when it's a good time to catch him,' he whispered.

The time came for the festival meal.
There was bread and wine on the
table. Jesus took each in turn and
shared it with his twelve friends.

'Tonight, God is making a
promise,' he said.

'It's a promise for everyone who
follows me and obeys me. One day,
you will eat and drink at my table
in my kingdom.'

His friends didn't really understand.
They just talked noisily. Except for
Judas, who slipped away.

After the meal, Jesus and the rest of his friends went to a quiet hillside. It was night. The olive trees cast dark shadows.

Alone and quietly, Jesus prayed to God.

'I know that terrible things are about to happen,' he prayed. 'I wish there were another way to make everything work out… but there isn't.'

Suddenly, Judas arrived.
   With him were some of the people
in charge of the Temple and some
of the Temple guards.

They took Jesus away. They paid
people to tell lies about him and say
he had done wrong things.

They marched him off to the ruler
of Jerusalem, who was called
Pontius Pilate.

'This Jesus is a rebel – he does wrong things,' they said. 'He must die.'

Pilate didn't really believe them. 'Is that what you and the people really want?' he asked.

'Yes it is,' everyone shouted. 'Crucify him!'

Pilate gave the order for Jesus to die.

Soldiers took Jesus away and nailed him to a cross.

From the cross Jesus said a prayer.

'Forgive them, Father! They don't know what they are doing.'

He looked at the people standing nearby. There was his mother, Mary, and next to her, his loyal friend John.

'Please take care of my mother when I'm gone,' said Jesus. John nodded, and put his arm round Mary.

The hours went by. Jesus died on the cross. A man named Joseph came and took the body.

He and his helpers laid it in a tomb that was like a cave.

The tomb had a round stone door. They rolled it shut. They had to hurry, because the weekly day of rest began at sunset.

The day after the day of rest was Sunday.

Some of the women who had followed Jesus came back to the tomb.

'What has happened?' they cried. 'Why is the door open?'

'Why is the tomb empty?'

Suddenly, two people in bright shining clothes appeared.

'Jesus isn't here,' they said. 'He's alive again.'

Not long after, they all saw him
alive again.

'My work is done,' said Jesus.
'You have listened to everything
I told you about God. You have
seen miracles. You have seen me
alive again.

'Now you must go and
tell the world about all
you have learned.

'God will make you
wise and brave.'

Then he said a blessing
prayer and was taken
up into heaven.

Jesus' followers didn't feel wise or
brave. They wanted to hide indoors.
  Then came the festival called
Pentecost. Early in the morning,
when they were indoors together,
they heard a noise like a strong
wind blowing.

They saw something like flames of fire dancing overhead.

Suddenly, they knew for sure that God was with them.

They hurried out to tell all the world about Jesus and his message.

The news is still spreading.